This book belongs to:

My roots

4.

Birth date:
Birth place:
Ocupation:
Married date:
Married location:
Death date:
Death location:
Buried location:

2.Father

Birth date:
Birth place:
Ocupation:
Married date:
Married location:
Death date:
Death location:
Buried location:

5.

Birth date:
Birth place:
Ocupation:
Death date:
Death location:
Buried location:

1.

Birth date:
Birth place:
Ocupation:
Married date:
Married location:
Death date:
Death location:
Buried location:

6.

Birth date:
Birth place:
Ocupation:
Married date:
Married location:
Death date:
Death location:
Buried location:

3.Mother

Birth date:
Birth place:
Ocupation:
Death date:
Death location:
Buried location:

7.

Birth date:
Birth place:
Ocupation:
Death date:
Death location:
Buried location:

8.

Birth date:
Birth place:
Ocupation:
Married date:
Married location:
Death date:
Death location:
Buried location:

9.

Birth date:
Birth place:
Death date:
Death location:
Buried location:

10.

Birth date:
Birth place:
Ocupation:
Married date:
Married location:
Death date:
Death location:
Buried location:

11.

Birth date:
Birth place:
Death date:
Death location:
Buried location:

12.

Birth date:
Birth place:
Ocupation:
Married date:
Married location:
Death date:
Death location:
Buried location:

13.

Birth date:
Birth place:
Death date:
Death location:
Buried location:

14.

Birth date:
Birth place:
Ocupation:
Married date:
Married location:
Death date:
Death location:
Buried location:

15.

Birth date:
Birth place:
Death date:
Death location:
Buried location:

16.

Birth date:	Married location:	Buried location:
Birth place:	Death date:	
Married date:	Date location:	

17.

| Birth date: | Death date: | Buried location: |
| Birth place: | Date location: | |

18.

Birth date:	Married location:	Buried location:
Birth place:	Death date:	
Married date:	Date location:	

19.

| Birth date: | Death date: | Buried location: |
| Birth place: | Date location: | |

20.

Birth date:	Married location:	Buried location:
Birth place:	Death date:	
Married date:	Date location:	

21.

| Birth date: | Death date: | Buried location: |
| Birth place: | Date location: | |

22.

Birth date:	Married location:	Buried location:
Birth place:	Death date:	
Married date:	Date location:	

23.

| Birth date: | Death date: | Buried location: |
| Birth place: | Date location: | |

24.

Birth date:	Married location:	Buried location:
Birth place:	Death date:	
Married date:	Date location:	

25.

| Birth date: | Death date: | Buried location: |
| Birth place: | Date location: | |

26.

Birth date:	Married location:	Buried location:
Birth place:	Death date:	
Married date:	Date location:	

27.

| Birth date: | Death date: | Buried location: |
| Birth place: | Date location: | |

28.

Birth date:	Married location:	Buried location:
Birth place:	Death date:	
Married date:	Date location:	

29.

| Birth date: | Death date: | Buried location: |
| Birth place: | Date location: | |

30.

Birth date:	Married location:	Buried location:
Birth place:	Death date:	
Married date:	Date location:	

31.

| Birth date: | Death date: | Buried location: |
| Birth place: | Date location: | |

My roots

4.

Birth date:
Birth place:
Ocupation:
Married date:
Married location:
Death date:
Death location:
Buried location:

2.Father

Birth date:
Birth place:
Ocupation:
Married date:
Married location:
Death date:
Death location:
Buried location:

5.

Birth date:
Birth place:
Ocupation:
Death date:
Death location:
Buried location:

1.

Birth date:
Birth place:
Ocupation:
Married date:
Married location:
Death date:
Death location:
Buried location:

6.

Birth date:
Birth place:
Ocupation:
Married date:
Married location:
Death date:
Death location:
Buried location:

3.Mother

Birth date:
Birth place:
Ocupation:
Death date:
Death location:
Buried location:

7.

Birth date:
Birth place:
Ocupation:
Death date:
Death location:
Buried location:

8.

Birth date:
Birth place:
Ocupation:
Married date:
Married location:
Death date:
Death location:
Buried location:

9.

Birth date:
Birth place:
Death date:
Death location:
Buried location:

10.

Birth date:
Birth place:
Ocupation:
Married date:
Married location:
Death date:
Death location:
Buried location:

11.

Birth date:
Birth place:
Death date:
Death location:
Buried location:

12.

Birth date:
Birth place:
Ocupation:
Married date:
Married location:
Death date:
Death location:
Buried location:

13.

Birth date:
Birth place:
Death date:
Death location:
Buried location:

14.

Birth date:
Birth place:
Ocupation:
Married date:
Married location:
Death date:
Death location:
Buried location:

15.

Birth date:
Birth place:
Death date:
Death location:
Buried location:

16.

Birth date: Married location: Buried location:
Birth place: Death date:
Married date: Date location:

17.

Birth date: Death date: Buried location:
Birth place: Date location:

18.

Birth date: Married location: Buried location:
Birth place: Death date:
Married date: Date location:

19.

Birth date: Death date: Buried location:
Birth place: Date location:

20.

Birth date: Married location: Buried location:
Birth place: Death date:
Married date: Date location:

21.

Birth date: Death date: Buried location:
Birth place: Date location:

22.

Birth date: Married location: Buried location:
Birth place: Death date:
Married date: Date location:

23.

Birth date: Death date: Buried location:
Birth place: Date location:

24.

Birth date: Married location: Buried location:
Birth place: Death date:
Married date: Date location:

25.

Birth date: Death date: Buried location:
Birth place: Date location:

26.

Birth date: Married location: Buried location:
Birth place: Death date:
Married date: Date location:

27.

Birth date: Death date: Buried location:
Birth place: Date location:

28.

Birth date: Married location: Buried location:
Birth place: Death date:
Married date: Date location:

29.

Birth date: Death date: Buried location:
Birth place: Date location:

30.

Birth date: Married location: Buried location:
Birth place: Death date:
Married date: Date location:

31.

Birth date: Death date: Buried location:
Birth place: Date location:

My roots

4.

Birth date:
Birth place:
Ocupation:
Married date:
Married location:
Death date:
Death location:
Buried location:

2.Father

Birth date:
Birth place:
Ocupation:
Married date:
Married location:
Death date:
Death location:
Buried location:

5.

Birth date:
Birth place:
Ocupation:
Death date:
Death location:
Buried location:

1.

Birth date:
Birth place:
Ocupation:
Married date:
Married location:
Death date:
Death location:
Buried location:

6.

Birth date:
Birth place:
Ocupation:
Married date:
Married location:
Death date:
Death location:
Buried location:

3.Mother

Birth date:
Birth place:
Ocupation:
Death date:
Death location:
Buried location:

7.

Birth date:
Birth place:
Ocupation:
Death date:
Death location:
Buried location:

8.

Birth date:
Birth place:
Ocupation:
Married date:
Married location:
Death date:
Death location:
Buried location:

9.

Birth date:
Birth place:
Death date:
Death location:
Buried location:

10.

Birth date:
Birth place:
Ocupation:
Married date:
Married location:
Death date:
Death location:
Buried location:

11.

Birth date:
Birth place:
Death date:
Death location:
Buried location:

12.

Birth date:
Birth place:
Ocupation:
Married date:
Married location:
Death date:
Death location:
Buried location:

13.

Birth date:
Birth place:
Death date:
Death location:
Buried location:

14.

Birth date:
Birth place:
Ocupation:
Married date:
Married location:
Death date:
Death location:
Buried location:

15.

Birth date:
Birth place:
Death date:
Death location:
Buried location:

16.

Birth date:	Married location:	Buried location:
Birth place:	Death date:	
Married date:	Date location:	

17.

| Birth date: | Death date: | Buried location: |
| Birth place: | Date location: | |

18.

Birth date:	Married location:	Buried location:
Birth place:	Death date:	
Married date:	Date location:	

19.

| Birth date: | Death date: | Buried location: |
| Birth place: | Date location: | |

20.

Birth date:	Married location:	Buried location:
Birth place:	Death date:	
Married date:	Date location:	

21.

| Birth date: | Death date: | Buried location: |
| Birth place: | Date location: | |

22.

Birth date:	Married location:	Buried location:
Birth place:	Death date:	
Married date:	Date location:	

23.

| Birth date: | Death date: | Buried location: |
| Birth place: | Date location: | |

24.

Birth date:	Married location:	Buried location:
Birth place:	Death date:	
Married date:	Date location:	

25.

| Birth date: | Death date: | Buried location: |
| Birth place: | Date location: | |

26.

Birth date:	Married location:	Buried location:
Birth place:	Death date:	
Married date:	Date location:	

27.

| Birth date: | Death date: | Buried location: |
| Birth place: | Date location: | |

28.

Birth date:	Married location:	Buried location:
Birth place:	Death date:	
Married date:	Date location:	

29.

| Birth date: | Death date: | Buried location: |
| Birth place: | Date location: | |

30.

Birth date:	Married location:	Buried location:
Birth place:	Death date:	
Married date:	Date location:	

31.

| Birth date: | Death date: | Buried location: |
| Birth place: | Date location: | |

My roots

4.

Birth date:
Birth place:
Ocupation:
Married date:
Married location:
Death date:
Death location:
Buried location:

2.Father

Birth date:
Birth place:
Ocupation:
Married date:
Married location:
Death date:
Death location:
Buried location:

5.

Birth date:
Birth place:
Ocupation:
Death date:
Death location:
Buried location:

1.

Birth date:
Birth place:
Ocupation:
Married date:
Married location:
Death date:
Death location:
Buried location:

6.

Birth date:
Birth place:
Ocupation:
Married date:
Married location:
Death date:
Death location:
Buried location:

3.Mother

Birth date:
Birth place:
Ocupation:
Death date:
Death location:
Buried location:

7.

Birth date:
Birth place:
Ocupation:
Death date:
Death location:
Buried location:

8.

Birth date:
Birth place:
Ocupation:
Married date:
Married location:
Death date:
Death location:
Buried location:

9.

Birth date:
Birth place:
Death date:
Death location:
Buried location:

10.

Birth date:
Birth place:
Ocupation:
Married date:
Married location:
Death date:
Death location:
Buried location:

11.

Birth date:
Birth place:
Death date:
Death location:
Buried location:

12.

Birth date:
Birth place:
Ocupation:
Married date:
Married location:
Death date:
Death location:
Buried location:

13.

Birth date:
Birth place:
Death date:
Death location:
Buried location:

14.

Birth date:
Birth place:
Ocupation:
Married date:
Married location:
Death date:
Death location:
Buried location:

15.

Birth date:
Birth place:
Death date:
Death location:
Buried location:

16.

Birth date:	Married location:	Buried location:
Birth place:	Death date:	
Married date:	Date location:	

17.

| Birth date: | Death date: | Buried location: |
| Birth place: | Date location: | |

18.

Birth date:	Married location:	Buried location:
Birth place:	Death date:	
Married date:	Date location:	

19.

| Birth date: | Death date: | Buried location: |
| Birth place: | Date location: | |

20.

Birth date:	Married location:	Buried location:
Birth place:	Death date:	
Married date:	Date location:	

21.

| Birth date: | Death date: | Buried location: |
| Birth place: | Date location: | |

22.

Birth date:	Married location:	Buried location:
Birth place:	Death date:	
Married date:	Date location:	

23.

| Birth date: | Death date: | Buried location: |
| Birth place: | Date location: | |

24.

Birth date:	Married location:	Buried location:
Birth place:	Death date:	
Married date:	Date location:	

25.

| Birth date: | Death date: | Buried location: |
| Birth place: | Date location: | |

26.

Birth date:	Married location:	Buried location:
Birth place:	Death date:	
Married date:	Date location:	

27.

| Birth date: | Death date: | Buried location: |
| Birth place: | Date location: | |

28.

Birth date:	Married location:	Buried location:
Birth place:	Death date:	
Married date:	Date location:	

29.

| Birth date: | Death date: | Buried location: |
| Birth place: | Date location: | |

30.

Birth date:	Married location:	Buried location:
Birth place:	Death date:	
Married date:	Date location:	

31.

| Birth date: | Death date: | Buried location: |
| Birth place: | Date location: | |

My roots

4.

Birth date:
Birth place:
Ocupation:
Married date:
Married location:
Death date:
Death location:
Buried location:

2.Father

Birth date:
Birth place:
Ocupation:
Married date:
Married location:
Death date:
Death location:
Buried location:

5.

Birth date:
Birth place:
Ocupation:
Death date:
Death location:
Buried location:

1.

Birth date:
Birth place:
Ocupation:
Married date:
Married location:
Death date:
Death location:
Buried location:

6.

Birth date:
Birth place:
Ocupation:
Married date:
Married location:
Death date:
Death location:
Buried location:

3.Mother

Birth date:
Birth place:
Ocupation:
Death date:
Death location:
Buried location:

7.

Birth date:
Birth place:
Ocupation:
Death date:
Death location:
Buried location:

8.

Birth date:
Birth place:
Ocupation:
Married date:
Married location:
Death date:
Death location:
Buried location:

9.

Birth date:
Birth place:
Death date:
Death location:
Buried location:

10.

Birth date:
Birth place:
Ocupation:
Married date:
Married location:
Death date:
Death location:
Buried location:

11.

Birth date:
Birth place:
Death date:
Death location:
Buried location:

12.

Birth date:
Birth place:
Ocupation:
Married date:
Married location:
Death date:
Death location:
Buried location:

13.

Birth date:
Birth place:
Death date:
Death location:
Buried location:

14.

Birth date:
Birth place:
Ocupation:
Married date:
Married location:
Death date:
Death location:
Buried location:

15.

Birth date:
Birth place:
Death date:
Death location:
Buried location:

16.

Birth date:	Married location:	Buried location:
Birth place:	Death date:	
Married date:	Date location:	

17.

Birth date:	Death date:	Buried location:
Birth place:	Date location:	

18.

Birth date:	Married location:	Buried location:
Birth place:	Death date:	
Married date:	Date location:	

19.

Birth date:	Death date:	Buried location:
Birth place:	Date location:	

20.

Birth date:	Married location:	Buried location:
Birth place:	Death date:	
Married date:	Date location:	

21.

Birth date:	Death date:	Buried location:
Birth place:	Date location:	

22.

Birth date:	Married location:	Buried location:
Birth place:	Death date:	
Married date:	Date location:	

23.

Birth date:	Death date:	Buried location:
Birth place:	Date location:	

24.

Birth date:	Married location:	Buried location:
Birth place:	Death date:	
Married date:	Date location:	

25.

Birth date:	Death date:	Buried location:
Birth place:	Date location:	

26.

Birth date:	Married location:	Buried location:
Birth place:	Death date:	
Married date:	Date location:	

27.

Birth date:	Death date:	Buried location:
Birth place:	Date location:	

28.

Birth date:	Married location:	Buried location:
Birth place:	Death date:	
Married date:	Date location:	

29.

Birth date:	Death date:	Buried location:
Birth place:	Date location:	

30.

Birth date:	Married location:	Buried location:
Birth place:	Death date:	
Married date:	Date location:	

31.

Birth date:	Death date:	Buried location:
Birth place:	Date location:	

My roots

4.

Birth date:
Birth place:
Ocupation:
Married date:
Married location:
Death date:
Death location:
Buried location:

2.Father

Birth date:
Birth place:
Ocupation:
Married date:
Married location:
Death date:
Death location:
Buried location:

5.

Birth date:
Birth place:
Ocupation:
Death date:
Death location:
Buried location:

1.

Birth date:
Birth place:
Ocupation:
Married date:
Married location:
Death date:
Death location:
Buried location:

6.

Birth date:
Birth place:
Ocupation:
Married date:
Married location:
Death date:
Death location:
Buried location:

3.Mother

Birth date:
Birth place:
Ocupation:
Death date:
Death location:
Buried location:

7.

Birth date:
Birth place:
Ocupation:
Death date:
Death location:
Buried location:

8.

Birth date:
Birth place:
Ocupation:
Married date:
Married location:
Death date:
Death location:
Buried location:

9.

Birth date:
Birth place:
Death date:
Death location:
Buried location:

10.

Birth date:
Birth place:
Ocupation:
Married date:
Married location:
Death date:
Death location:
Buried location:

11.

Birth date:
Birth place:
Death date:
Death location:
Buried location:

12.

Birth date:
Birth place:
Ocupation:
Married date:
Married location:
Death date:
Death location:
Buried location:

13.

Birth date:
Birth place:
Death date:
Death location:
Buried location:

14.

Birth date:
Birth place:
Ocupation:
Married date:
Married location:
Death date:
Death location:
Buried location:

15.

Birth date:
Birth place:
Death date:
Death location:
Buried location:

16.

Birth date:	Married location:	Buried location:
Birth place:	Death date:	
Married date:	Date location:	

17.

| Birth date: | Death date: | Buried location: |
| Birth place: | Date location: | |

18.

Birth date:	Married location:	Buried location:
Birth place:	Death date:	
Married date:	Date location:	

19.

| Birth date: | Death date: | Buried location: |
| Birth place: | Date location: | |

20.

Birth date:	Married location:	Buried location:
Birth place:	Death date:	
Married date:	Date location:	

21.

| Birth date: | Death date: | Buried location: |
| Birth place: | Date location: | |

22.

Birth date:	Married location:	Buried location:
Birth place:	Death date:	
Married date:	Date location:	

23.

| Birth date: | Death date: | Buried location: |
| Birth place: | Date location: | |

24.

Birth date:	Married location:	Buried location:
Birth place:	Death date:	
Married date:	Date location:	

25.

| Birth date: | Death date: | Buried location: |
| Birth place: | Date location: | |

26.

Birth date:	Married location:	Buried location:
Birth place:	Death date:	
Married date:	Date location:	

27.

| Birth date: | Death date: | Buried location: |
| Birth place: | Date location: | |

28.

Birth date:	Married location:	Buried location:
Birth place:	Death date:	
Married date:	Date location:	

29.

| Birth date: | Death date: | Buried location: |
| Birth place: | Date location: | |

30.

Birth date:	Married location:	Buried location:
Birth place:	Death date:	
Married date:	Date location:	

31.

| Birth date: | Death date: | Buried location: |
| Birth place: | Date location: | |

Family Group

HUSBAND

First Name:	Middle Name:
Last Name:	Nickname:
Birthdate:	Birthplace:
Marriage Date:	Marriage Place:
Death Date:	Death Place:
Other Wives:	
Other Spouse Children:	
Father's Name:	Mother's Name:

This person is number .... on chart #..........

WIFE

First Name:	Middle Name:
Last Name:	Nickname:
Birthdate:	Birthplace:
Death Date:	Death Place:
Other Husbands:	
Other Spouse Children:	
Father's Name:	Mother's Name:

This person is number .... on chart #..........

SIBLINGS

Name	Related to	Birthdate/place	Spouse	Children	Death Date/Place
1.					
2.					
3.					
4.					
5.					
6.					
7.					
8.					
9.					
10.					

CHILDREN

Name	Birthdate/place	Marriage Date/Place	Spouse	Children	Death Date/Place
1.					
2.					
3.					
4.					
5.					
6.					
7.					
8.					
9.					
10.					

Family Group

HUSBAND

First Name:	Middle Name:
Last Name:	Nickname:
Birthdate:	Birthplace:
Marriage Date:	Marriage Place:
Death Date:	Death Place:
Other Wives:	
Other Spouse Children:	
Father's Name:	Mother's Name:

This person is number .... on chart #..........

WIFE

First Name:	Middle Name:
Last Name:	Nickname:
Birthdate:	Birthplace:
Death Date:	Death Place:
Other Husbands:	
Other Spouse Children:	
Father's Name:	Mother's Name:

This person is number .... on chart #..........

SIBLINGS

Name	Related to	Birthdate/place	Spouse	Children	Death Date/Place
1.					
2.					
3.					
4.					
5.					
6.					
7.					
8.					
9.					
10.					

CHILDREN

Name	Birthdate/place	Marriage Date/Place	Spouse	Children	Death Date/Place
1.					
2.					
3.					
4.					
5.					
6.					
7.					
8.					
9.					
10.					

Family Group

HUSBAND

First Name:	Middle Name:
Last Name:	Nickname:
Birthdate:	Birthplace:
Marriage Date:	Marriage Place:
Death Date:	Death Place:
Other Wives:	
Other Spouse Children:	
Father's Name:	Mother's Name:

This person is number .... on chart #..........

WIFE

First Name:	Middle Name:
Last Name:	Nickname:
Birthdate:	Birthplace:
Death Date:	Death Place:
Other Husbands:	
Other Spouse Children:	
Father's Name:	Mother's Name:

This person is number .... on chart #..........

SIBLINGS

Name	Related to	Birthdate/place	Spouse	Children	Death Date/Place
1.					
2.					
3.					
4.					
5.					
6.					
7.					
8.					
9.					
10.					

CHILDREN

Name	Birthdate/place	Marriage Date/Place	Spouse	Children	Death Date/Place
1.					
2.					
3.					
4.					
5.					
6.					
7.					
8.					
9.					
10.					

Family Group

HUSBAND

First Name:	Middle Name:
Last Name:	Nickname:
Birthdate:	Birthplace:
Marriage Date:	Marriage Place:
Death Date:	Death Place:
Other Wives:	
Other Spouse Children:	
Father's Name:	Mother's Name:

This person is number .... on chart #..........

WIFE

First Name:	Middle Name:
Last Name:	Nickname:
Birthdate:	Birthplace:
Death Date:	Death Place:
Other Husbands:	
Other Spouse Children:	
Father's Name:	Mother's Name:

This person is number .... on chart #..........

SIBLINGS

	Name	Related to	Birthdate/place	Spouse	Children	Death Date/Place
1.						
2.						
3.						
4.						
5.						
6.						
7.						
8.						
9.						
10.						

CHILDREN

	Name	Birthdate/place	Marriage Date/Place	Spouse	Children	Death Date/Place
1.						
2.						
3.						
4.						
5.						
6.						
7.						
8.						
9.						
10.						

Family Group

HUSBAND

First Name:	Middle Name:
Last Name:	Nickname:
Birthdate:	Birthplace:
Marriage Date:	Marriage Place:
Death Date:	Death Place:
Other Wives:	
Other Spouse Children:	
Father's Name:	Mother's Name:

This person is number .... on chart #..........

WIFE

First Name:	Middle Name:
Last Name:	Nickname:
Birthdate:	Birthplace:
Death Date:	Death Place:
Other Husbands:	
Other Spouse Children:	
Father's Name:	Mother's Name:

This person is number .... on chart #..........

SIBLINGS

Name	Related to	Birthdate/place	Spouse	Children	Death Date/Place
1.					
2.					
3.					
4.					
5.					
6.					
7.					
8.					
9.					
10.					

CHILDREN

Name	Birthdate/place	Marriage Date/Place	Spouse	Children	Death Date/Place
1.					
2.					
3.					
4.					
5.					
6.					
7.					
8.					
9.					
10.					

Family Group

HUSBAND

First Name:	Middle Name:
Last Name:	Nickname:
Birthdate:	Birthplace:
Marriage Date:	Marriage Place:
Death Date:	Death Place:
Other Wives:	
Other Spouse Children:	
Father's Name:	Mother's Name:

This person is number .... on chart #..........

WIFE

First Name:	Middle Name:
Last Name:	Nickname:
Birthdate:	Birthplace:
Death Date:	Death Place:
Other Husbands:	
Other Spouse Children:	
Father's Name:	Mother's Name:

This person is number .... on chart #..........

SIBLINGS

Name	Related to	Birthdate/place	Spouse	Children	Death Date/Place
1.					
2.					
3.					
4.					
5.					
6.					
7.					
8.					
9.					
10.					

CHILDREN

Name	Birthdate/place	Marriage Date/Place	Spouse	Children	Death Date/Place
1.					
2.					
3.					
4.					
5.					
6.					
7.					
8.					
9.					
10.					

Family Group

HUSBAND

First Name:	Middle Name:
Last Name:	Nickname:
Birthdate:	Birthplace:
Marriage Date:	Marriage Place:
Death Date:	Death Place:
Other Wives:	
Other Spouse Children:	
Father's Name:	Mother's Name:

This person is number .... on chart #..........

WIFE

First Name:	Middle Name:
Last Name:	Nickname:
Birthdate:	Birthplace:
Death Date:	Death Place:
Other Husbands:	
Other Spouse Children:	
Father's Name:	Mother's Name:

This person is number .... on chart #..........

SIBLINGS

	Name	Related to	Birthdate/place	Spouse	Children	Death Date/Place
1.						
2.						
3.						
4.						
5.						
6.						
7.						
8.						
9.						
10.						

CHILDREN

	Name	Birthdate/place	Marriage Date/Place	Spouse	Children	Death Date/Place
1.						
2.						
3.						
4.						
5.						
6.						
7.						
8.						
9.						
10.						

Family Group

HUSBAND

First Name:	Middle Name:
Last Name:	Nickname:
Birthdate:	Birthplace:
Marriage Date:	Marriage Place:
Death Date:	Death Place:
Other Wives:	
Other Spouse Children:	
Father's Name:	Mother's Name:

This person is number .... on chart #..........

WIFE

First Name:	Middle Name:
Last Name:	Nickname:
Birthdate:	Birthplace:
Death Date:	Death Place:
Other Husbands:	
Other Spouse Children:	
Father's Name:	Mother's Name:

This person is number .... on chart #..........

SIBLINGS

Name	Related to	Birthdate/place	Spouse	Children	Death Date/Place
1.					
2.					
3.					
4.					
5.					
6.					
7.					
8.					
9.					
10.					

CHILDREN

Name	Birthdate/place	Marriage Date/Place	Spouse	Children	Death Date/Place
1.					
2.					
3.					
4.					
5.					
6.					
7.					
8.					
9.					
10.					

Family Group

HUSBAND

First Name:	Middle Name:
Last Name:	Nickname:
Birthdate:	Birthplace:
Marriage Date:	Marriage Place:
Death Date:	Death Place:
Other Wives:	
Other Spouse Children:	
Father's Name:	Mother's Name:

This person is number .... on chart #..........

WIFE

First Name:	Middle Name:
Last Name:	Nickname:
Birthdate:	Birthplace:
Death Date:	Death Place:
Other Husbands:	
Other Spouse Children:	
Father's Name:	Mother's Name:

This person is number .... on chart #..........

SIBLINGS

Name	Related to	Birthdate/place	Spouse	Children	Death Date/Place
1.					
2.					
3.					
4.					
5.					
6.					
7.					
8.					
9.					
10.					

CHILDREN

Name	Birthdate/place	Marriage Date/Place	Spouse	Children	Death Date/Place
1.					
2.					
3.					
4.					
5.					
6.					
7.					
8.					
9.					
10.					

Family Group

HUSBAND

First Name:	Middle Name:
Last Name:	Nickname:
Birthdate:	Birthplace:
Marriage Date:	Marriage Place:
Death Date:	Death Place:
Other Wives:	
Other Spouse Children:	
Father's Name:	Mother's Name:

This person is number ……. on chart #……….

WIFE

First Name:	Middle Name:
Last Name:	Nickname:
Birthdate:	Birthplace:
Death Date:	Death Place:
Other Husbands:	
Other Spouse Children:	
Father's Name:	Mother's Name:

This person is number ……. on chart #……….

SIBLINGS

Name	Related to	Birthdate/place	Spouse	Children	Death Date/Place
1.					
2.					
3.					
4.					
5.					
6.					
7.					
8.					
9.					
10.					

CHILDREN

Name	Birthdate/place	Marriage Date/Place	Spouse	Children	Death Date/Place
1.					
2.					
3.					
4.					
5.					
6.					
7.					
8.					
9.					
10.					

Family Group

HUSBAND

First Name:	Middle Name:
Last Name:	Nickname:
Birthdate:	Birthplace:
Marriage Date:	Marriage Place:
Death Date:	Death Place:
Other Wives:	
Other Spouse Children:	
Father's Name:	Mother's Name:

This person is number .... on chart #..........

WIFE

First Name:	Middle Name:
Last Name:	Nickname:
Birthdate:	Birthplace:
Death Date:	Death Place:
Other Husbands:	
Other Spouse Children:	
Father's Name:	Mother's Name:

This person is number .... on chart #..........

SIBLINGS

Name	Related to	Birthdate/place	Spouse	Children	Death Date/Place
1.					
2.					
3.					
4.					
5.					
6.					
7.					
8.					
9.					
10.					

CHILDREN

Name	Birthdate/place	Marriage Date/Place	Spouse	Children	Death Date/Place
1.					
2.					
3.					
4.					
5.					
6.					
7.					
8.					
9.					
10.					

Family Group

HUSBAND

First Name:	Middle Name:
Last Name:	Nickname:
Birthdate:	Birthplace:
Marriage Date:	Marriage Place:
Death Date:	Death Place:
Other Wives:	
Other Spouse Children:	
Father's Name:	Mother's Name:

This person is number .... on chart #..........

WIFE

First Name:	Middle Name:
Last Name:	Nickname:
Birthdate:	Birthplace:
Death Date:	Death Place:
Other Husbands:	
Other Spouse Children:	
Father's Name:	Mother's Name:

This person is number .... on chart #..........

SIBLINGS

Name	Related to	Birthdate/place	Spouse	Children	Death Date/Place
1.					
2.					
3.					
4.					
5.					
6.					
7.					
8.					
9.					
10.					

CHILDREN

Name	Birthdate/place	Marriage Date/Place	Spouse	Children	Death Date/Place
1.					
2.					
3.					
4.					
5.					
6.					
7.					
8.					
9.					
10.					

Family Group

HUSBAND

First Name:	Middle Name:
Last Name:	Nickname:
Birthdate:	Birthplace:
Marriage Date:	Marriage Place:
Death Date:	Death Place:
Other Wives:	
Other Spouse Children:	
Father's Name:	Mother's Name:

This person is number .... on chart #..........

WIFE

First Name:	Middle Name:
Last Name:	Nickname:
Birthdate:	Birthplace:
Death Date:	Death Place:
Other Husbands:	
Other Spouse Children:	
Father's Name:	Mother's Name:

This person is number .... on chart #..........

SIBLINGS

Name	Related to	Birthdate/place	Spouse	Children	Death Date/Place
1.					
2.					
3.					
4.					
5.					
6.					
7.					
8.					
9.					
10.					

CHILDREN

Name	Birthdate/place	Marriage Date/Place	Spouse	Children	Death Date/Place
1.					
2.					
3.					
4.					
5.					
6.					
7.					
8.					
9.					
10.					

Family Group

HUSBAND

First Name:	Middle Name:
Last Name:	Nickname:
Birthdate:	Birthplace:
Marriage Date:	Marriage Place:
Death Date:	Death Place:
Other Wives:	
Other Spouse Children:	
Father's Name:	Mother's Name:

This person is number .... on chart #.........

WIFE

First Name:	Middle Name:
Last Name:	Nickname:
Birthdate:	Birthplace:
Death Date:	Death Place:
Other Husbands:	
Other Spouse Children:	
Father's Name:	Mother's Name:

This person is number .... on chart #.........

SIBLINGS

Name	Related to	Birthdate/place	Spouse	Children	Death Date/Place
1.					
2.					
3.					
4.					
5.					
6.					
7.					
8.					
9.					
10.					

CHILDREN

Name	Birthdate/place	Marriage Date/Place	Spouse	Children	Death Date/Place
1.					
2.					
3.					
4.					
5.					
6.					
7.					
8.					
9.					
10.					

Family Group

HUSBAND

First Name:	Middle Name:
Last Name:	Nickname:
Birthdate:	Birthplace:
Marriage Date:	Marriage Place:
Death Date:	Death Place:
Other Wives:	
Other Spouse Children:	
Father's Name:	Mother's Name:

This person is number .... on chart #..........

WIFE

First Name:	Middle Name:
Last Name:	Nickname:
Birthdate:	Birthplace:
Death Date:	Death Place:
Other Husbands:	
Other Spouse Children:	
Father's Name:	Mother's Name:

This person is number .... on chart #..........

SIBLINGS

Name	Related to	Birthdate/place	Spouse	Children	Death Date/Place
1.					
2.					
3.					
4.					
5.					
6.					
7.					
8.					
9.					
10.					

CHILDREN

Name	Birthdate/place	Marriage Date/Place	Spouse	Children	Death Date/Place
1.					
2.					
3.					
4.					
5.					
6.					
7.					
8.					
9.					
10.					

Family Group

HUSBAND

First Name:	Middle Name:
Last Name:	Nickname:
Birthdate:	Birthplace:
Marriage Date:	Marriage Place:
Death Date:	Death Place:
Other Wives:	
Other Spouse Children:	
Father's Name:	Mother's Name:

This person is number .... on chart #.........

WIFE

First Name:	Middle Name:
Last Name:	Nickname:
Birthdate:	Birthplace:
Death Date:	Death Place:
Other Husbands:	
Other Spouse Children:	
Father's Name:	Mother's Name:

This person is number .... on chart #.........

SIBLINGS

Name	Related to	Birthdate/place	Spouse	Children	Death Date/Place
1.					
2.					
3.					
4.					
5.					
6.					
7.					
8.					
9.					
10.					

CHILDREN

Name	Birthdate/place	Marriage Date/Place	Spouse	Children	Death Date/Place
1.					
2.					
3.					
4.					
5.					
6.					
7.					
8.					
9.					
10.					

Family Group

HUSBAND

First Name:	Middle Name:
Last Name:	Nickname:
Birthdate:	Birthplace:
Marriage Date:	Marriage Place:
Death Date:	Death Place:
Other Wives:	
Other Spouse Children:	
Father's Name:	Mother's Name:

This person is number .... on chart #..........

WIFE

First Name:	Middle Name:
Last Name:	Nickname:
Birthdate:	Birthplace:
Death Date:	Death Place:
Other Husbands:	
Other Spouse Children:	
Father's Name:	Mother's Name:

This person is number .... on chart #..........

SIBLINGS

Name	Related to	Birthdate/place	Spouse	Children	Death Date/Place
1.					
2.					
3.					
4.					
5.					
6.					
7.					
8.					
9.					
10.					

CHILDREN

Name	Birthdate/place	Marriage Date/Place	Spouse	Children	Death Date/Place
1.					
2.					
3.					
4.					
5.					
6.					
7.					
8.					
9.					
10.					

Family Group

HUSBAND

First Name:	Middle Name:
Last Name:	Nickname:
Birthdate:	Birthplace:
Marriage Date:	Marriage Place:
Death Date:	Death Place:
Other Wives:	
Other Spouse Children:	
Father's Name:	Mother's Name:

This person is number .... on chart #.........

WIFE

First Name:	Middle Name:
Last Name:	Nickname:
Birthdate:	Birthplace:
Death Date:	Death Place:
Other Husbands:	
Other Spouse Children:	
Father's Name:	Mother's Name:

This person is number .... on chart #.........

SIBLINGS

Name	Related to	Birthdate/place	Spouse	Children	Death Date/Place
1.					
2.					
3.					
4.					
5.					
6.					
7.					
8.					
9.					
10.					

CHILDREN

Name	Birthdate/place	Marriage Date/Place	Spouse	Children	Death Date/Place
1.					
2.					
3.					
4.					
5.					
6.					
7.					
8.					
9.					
10.					

Family Group

HUSBAND

First Name:	Middle Name:
Last Name:	Nickname:
Birthdate:	Birthplace:
Marriage Date:	Marriage Place:
Death Date:	Death Place:
Other Wives:	
Other Spouse Children:	
Father's Name:	Mother's Name:

This person is number .... on chart #..........

WIFE

First Name:	Middle Name:
Last Name:	Nickname:
Birthdate:	Birthplace:
Death Date:	Death Place:
Other Husbands:	
Other Spouse Children:	
Father's Name:	Mother's Name:

This person is number .... on chart #..........

SIBLINGS

	Name	Related to	Birthdate/place	Spouse	Children	Death Date/Place
1.						
2.						
3.						
4.						
5.						
6.						
7.						
8.						
9.						
10.						

CHILDREN

	Name	Birthdate/place	Marriage Date/Place	Spouse	Children	Death Date/Place
1.						
2.						
3.						
4.						
5.						
6.						
7.						
8.						
9.						
10.						

Family Group

HUSBAND

First Name:	Middle Name:
Last Name:	Nickname:
Birthdate:	Birthplace:
Marriage Date:	Marriage Place:
Death Date:	Death Place:
Other Wives:	
Other Spouse Children:	
Father's Name:	Mother's Name:

This person is number .... on chart #.........

WIFE

First Name:	Middle Name:
Last Name:	Nickname:
Birthdate:	Birthplace:
Death Date:	Death Place:
Other Husbands:	
Other Spouse Children:	
Father's Name:	Mother's Name:

This person is number .... on chart #.........

SIBLINGS

	Name	Related to	Birthdate/place	Spouse	Children	Death Date/Place
1.						
2.						
3.						
4.						
5.						
6.						
7.						
8.						
9.						
10.						

CHILDREN

	Name	Birthdate/place	Marriage Date/Place	Spouse	Children	Death Date/Place
1.						
2.						
3.						
4.						
5.						
6.						
7.						
8.						
9.						
10.						

Family Group

HUSBAND

First Name:	Middle Name:
Last Name:	Nickname:
Birthdate:	Birthplace:
Marriage Date:	Marriage Place:
Death Date:	Death Place:
Other Wives:	
Other Spouse Children:	
Father's Name:	Mother's Name:

This person is number .... on chart #..........

WIFE

First Name:	Middle Name:
Last Name:	Nickname:
Birthdate:	Birthplace:
Death Date:	Death Place:
Other Husbands:	
Other Spouse Children:	
Father's Name:	Mother's Name:

This person is number .... on chart #..........

SIBLINGS

Name	Related to	Birthdate/place	Spouse	Children	Death Date/Place
1.					
2.					
3.					
4.					
5.					
6.					
7.					
8.					
9.					
10.					

CHILDREN

Name	Birthdate/place	Marriage Date/Place	Spouse	Children	Death Date/Place
1.					
2.					
3.					
4.					
5.					
6.					
7.					
8.					
9.					
10.					

Cemetery Log

Name	Birth	Death	Age

Notes

Location in Cemetery				Head Stone		Date Researched
Section	Row	Lot	Grave	Artwork	Inscription	

Notes

Cemetery Log

Name	Birth	Death	Age

Notes

Location in Cemetery				Head Stone		Date Researched
Section	Row	Lot	Grave	Artwork	Inscription	

Notes

Cemetery Log

Name	Birth	Death	Age

Notes

Location in Cemetery				Head Stone		Date Researched
Section	Row	Lot	Grave	Artwork	Inscription	

Notes

Cemetery Log

Name	Birth	Death	Age

Notes

Location in Cemetery				Head Stone		Date Researched
Section	Row	Lot	Grave	Artwork	Inscription	

Notes

Cemetery Log

Name	Birth	Death	Age

Notes

Location in Cemetery				Head Stone		Date Researched
Section	Row	Lot	Grave	Artwork	Inscription	

Notes

Cemetery Log

Name	Birth	Death	Age

Notes

Location in Cemetery				Head Stone		Date Researched
Section	Row	Lot	Grave	Artwork	Inscription	

Notes

Research Checklist

Location	Documents	Taken Photo	Photo-copied

Notes

Research Checklist

Location	Documents	Taken Photo	Photo-copied

Notes

Research Checklist

Location	Documents	Taken Photo	Photo-copied

Notes

Research Checklist

Location	Documents	Taken Photo	Photo-copied

Notes

Research Checklist

Location	Documents	Taken Photo	Photo-copied

Notes

Research Checklist

Location	Documents	Taken Photo	Photo-copied

Notes

Notes

Notes

Notes

Notes

Notes

Notes

Notes

Notes

Notes

Notes

Notes

Notes

Notes

Notes

Notes

Notes

Notes

Notes

Notes

Notes

Notes

Notes

Notes

Notes

Notes

Notes

Photos

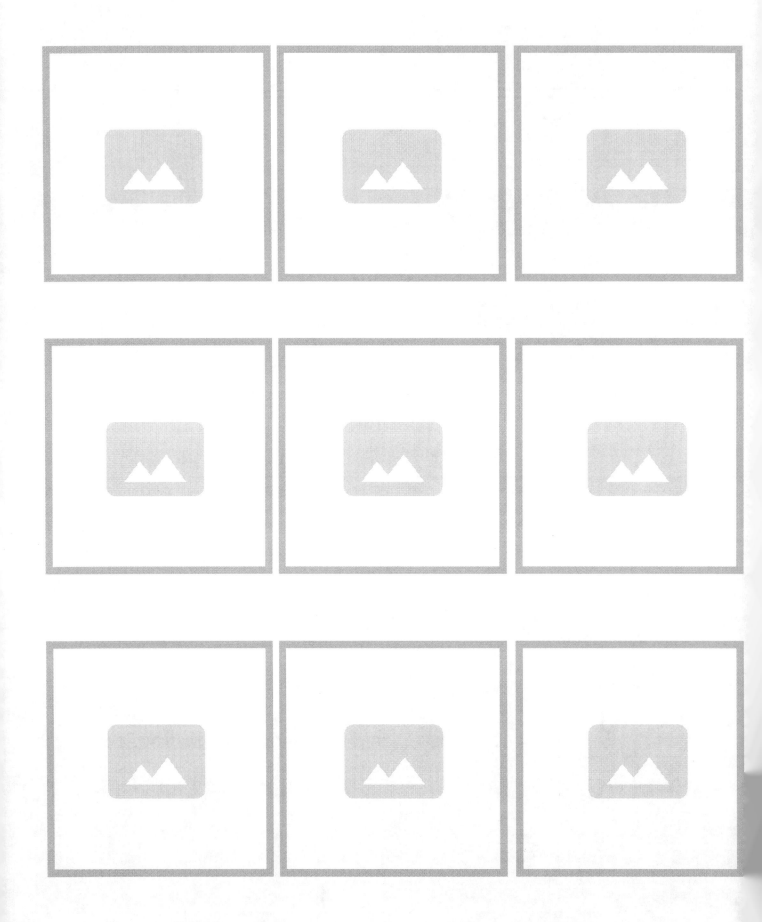

Photos

Photos

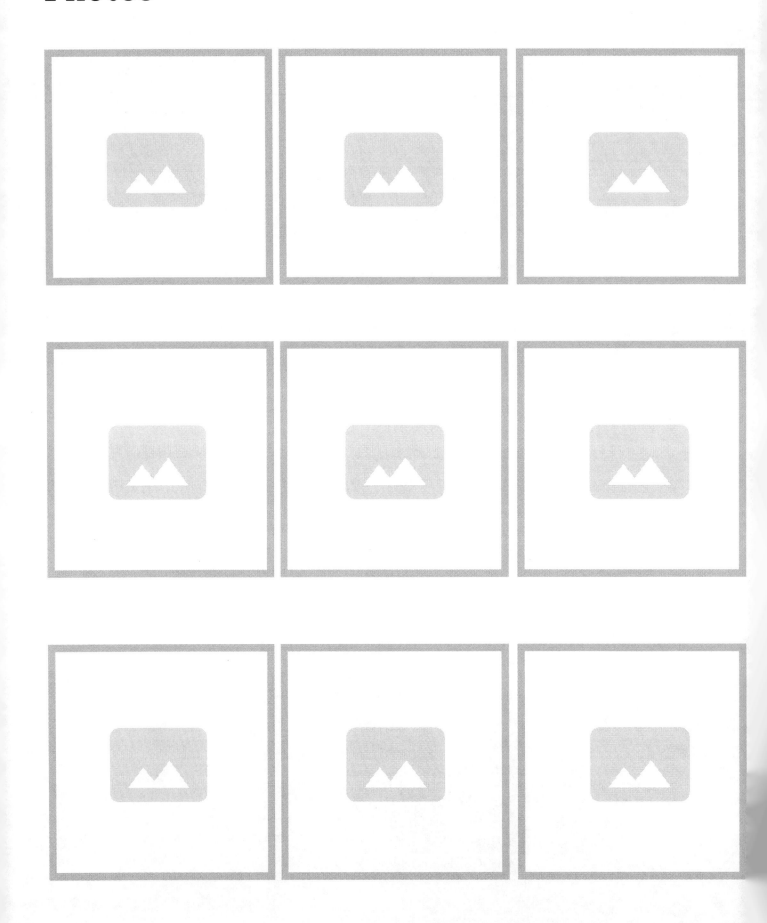

Photos

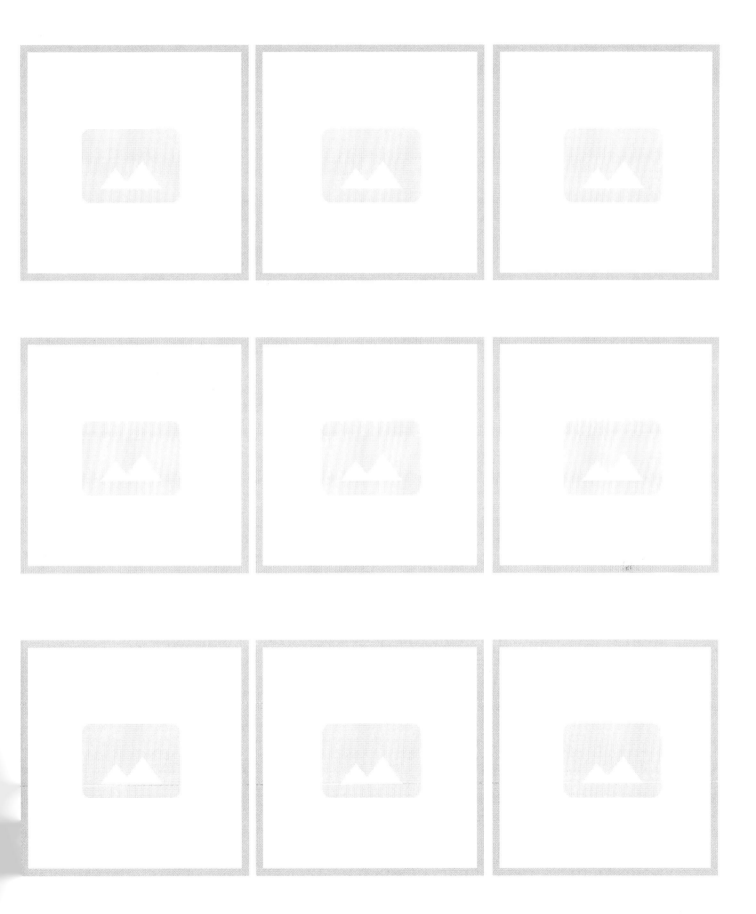

Photos

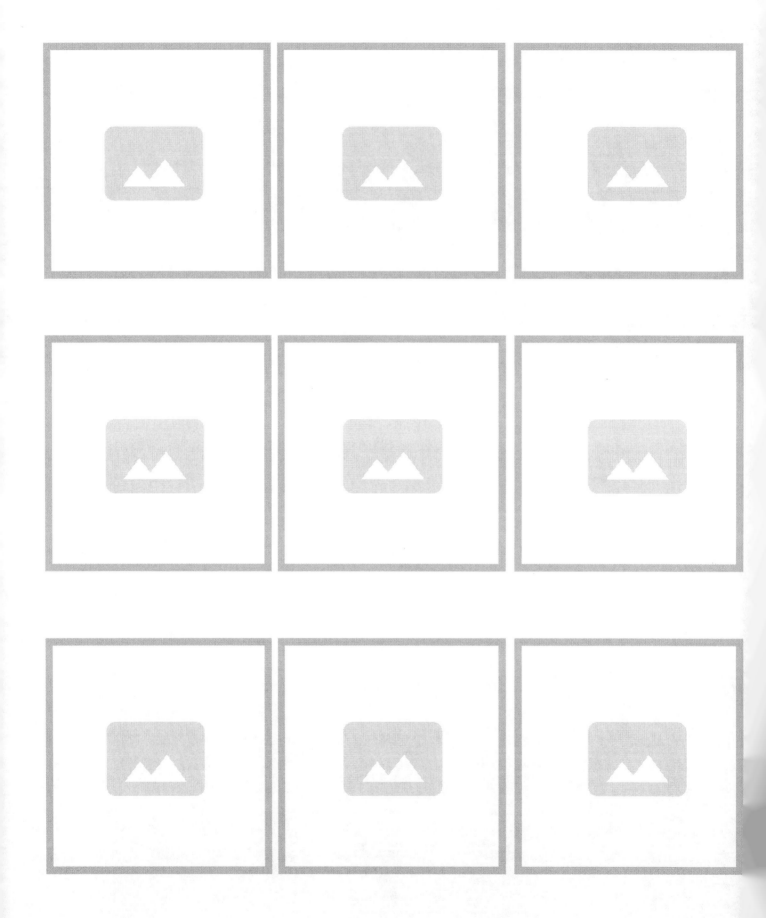

Photos

Made in the USA
Coppell, TX
30 September 2024

37865716R00059